THE GLASS WO.........
ROMAN LONDON

John Shepherd and Angela Wardle

with Mark Taylor and David Hill

Photography by Andy Chopping

MUSEUM OF LONDON ARCHAEOLOGY

First published in 2009 by
Museum of London Archaeology
46 Eagle Wharf Road, London N1 7ED
© Museum of London 2009

ISBN 978-1-901992-84-7

Text: John Shepherd and Angela Wardle
Edit: Sue Hirst
Photography and reprographics: Andy Chopping and Maggie Cox
Map: Carlos Lemos
Design and production: Tracy Wellman

ACKNOWLEDGEMENTS
Excavations at 35 Basinghall Street were carried out over a period
of seven months in 2005, conducted by Museum of London
Archaeology. The excavations were generously funded by Stanhope
PLC. Sophie Jackson was the MOLA project manager and Malcolm
MacKenzie the on-site project manager. David Bowsher is managing
the post-excavation work, which will include analysis of the site
findings and lead to the publication of a MOLA monograph on the
results of the excavation. Other important aspects will also appear
as academic papers elsewhere. The authors would particularly like to
thank Mark Taylor and David Hill for allowing their excellent work
reconstructing Roman glass-working techniques and furnaces to be
used in this book, and for the use of the figure on page 26. Thanks
also to Irena Lazar for permission to use the image of the Školarice-
Križišče lamp on page 9. This lamp is kept at the Regional Museum
Koper (Pokrajinski muzej Koper). The reconstruction painting on
page 30 is by Peter Froste.

COVER
Reheating a glass vessel at the mouth of the furnace

CONTENTS

INTRODUCTION

We often think of glassware as being a rare and luxury commodity in Roman Britain, but this impression is false. When the Romans invaded Britain in AD 43 glass vessels were indeed expensive items imported from the Continental glass workshops in Italy and Gaul. However, the invention of glass-blowing about a century before the Romans arrived in Britain meant that glass vessels could be mass-produced relatively cheaply and soon became commonplace. The explanation of why glass is thought of as rare is quite simple – so little of it is found. This rarity is not, however, due to its fragility, but rather to the important fact that it can be recycled.

Recycling may be a topical subject today, as we consider more ways to be energy-efficient and less wasteful, but it is by no means a new idea; throughout its long history glass has always been recycled. Evidence for this activity is now being found throughout the Roman Empire – and especially in Roman London, where a number of sites with evidence for the

A selection of 1st- and 2nd-century glass from Roman London

recycling of glass have been excavated. The latest discovery, and perhaps the most important in terms of the range of material found, was made in 2005 at 35 Basinghall Street, London, by Museum of London Archaeology (MOLA). Here the archaeologists discovered one of the largest dumps of glass waste ever found, from a glass-maker's workshop that was in use some 1800 years ago. This dump included thousands of fragments of broken glass vessels, cullet and production waste, which would normally have been remelted in a furnace and used to create new vessels. Among these fragments is important evidence for the ways in which vessels were made and what sort of vessels were being made. Exactly why this glass was never reused, but simply dumped and abandoned as rubbish, is hard to explain, but it is likely to coincide with the time when a glass workshop nearby went out of use.

This book tells the story of the discovery of this glass, how the study of this huge collection has taught us more about the glass workers of Roman London and what impact this discovery has had upon our general understanding of how glass vessels were made in Roman London.

But first let us briefly look at how glass is made, how it was used and the other evidence for its manufacture in the Roman town of Londinium.

Glass recycling today – a typical sight in 21st-century London

Roman cullet from the
Basinghall Street site

BEFORE WE BEGIN, JUST WHAT IS GLASS?

A Roman oil lamp showing glass workers around a furnace from Školarice-Križišče, Slovenia

The main ingredients of Roman glass were silica in the form of sand, soda, which was used as a flux to reduce the melting temperature of the mixture, and calcium in the form of lime, which acted as a stabiliser making the glass more durable. Soda, found in a natural form as natron, came from Egypt and it was in the eastern Mediterranean that raw glass was first made. Iron oxide, an impurity in sand, produces the characteristic blue-green shades of naturally-coloured Roman glass, but other minerals were added deliberately to give a variety of brilliant colours which were popular in the early 1st century AD. Manganese and antimony were added as decolourisers to produce the clear colourless vessels, which became fashionable in the later 1st century AD. As we will see, in London the glass workers probably made use of the colour resulting from simply remelting selected broken glass and did little in the way of colour alteration.

There is scant evidence that glass was ever made from the raw materials in Roman Britain and none at all from London. It was either imported from the Mediterranean in the form of large blocks or, alternatively, broken vessel and window glass, known as cullet, was collected for recycling. This was common practice throughout the Roman world, and broken vessel and window glass may actually have been traded – the 1st-century AD poet Martial records that it was exchanged for sulphur sticks that could be used as slow-burning matches. In Britain the collection of cullet would have become increasingly common as more glass, especially bottle glass, was imported, and became available for recycling. Recycling is environmentally friendly but can be archaeologically hostile, as the recycling of glass removes it from the archaeological record. Consequently discoveries of cullet, which contain a range of vessels in use at a specific point in time, are transforming our understanding both of the use of glass in Roman London, and also its glass-working industry. The largest dump of cullet ever found in Britain came from Guildhall Yard in London, south of Basinghall Street.

Detail of Roman cullet; broken glass vessels would have been collected from around the town and brought to the glass workshop for sorting; all the glass here is of one colour

Our knowledge about the structure of glass furnaces in London, and indeed elsewhere in the Roman world, is based on very limited evidence. A certain amount is known from a few excavated ground plans and some contemporary representations on lamps; the latter show furnaces with firing and melting chambers within a low domed superstructure. The evidence from London, such as it is, suggests that glass was prepared for blowing in a tank furnace, that is, in a reservoir in a furnace and not in crucibles more familiar from later glass working traditions. These tank furnaces were built of brickearth and contained a tank, rectangular in shape, made of pre-fired bricks and tiles suspended over a firebox, although there seems to have been some variation in the positioning of the tank within the furnace. There is as yet only very tenuous evidence, in the later Roman period, for the use of crucibles for melting the glass. At Basinghall we have only the glass from the furnace, known as tank metal, with a few fragments of tile, but nearby at 55–61 Moorgate and at Northgate House, Moorgate, substantial fragments of furnace structures were found.

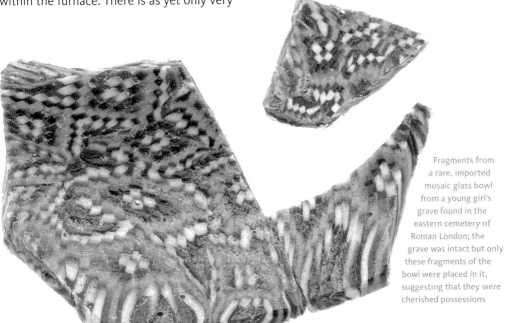

Fragments from a rare, imported mosaic glass bowl from a young girl's grave found in the eastern cemetery of Roman London; the grave was intact but only these fragments of the bowl were placed in it, suggesting that they were cherished possessions

David Hill and Mark Taylor, makers of replica Roman glass vessels, have carried out extensive work with experimental furnaces, and although in recent projects they have used heavy crucibles, rather than tank furnaces, many of the features seen and the waste produced by their work can be observed in the ancient Basinghall Street material. Such experimental work will be crucial to our understanding of the ancient processes. The picture above shows one of their furnaces at work. The crucibles can be clearly seen surrounded by the heat of the flames. Details, such as the vent or spy-hole plug (right), match specimens found on sites in London. After the furnace has cooled (far right), we are able to compare the fragments of the structure with the debris recovered from archaeological sites.

HOW DO YOU MAKE A GLASS VESSEL?

A vessel still attached to its blowing iron

Reheating a vessel at the mouth of the furnace

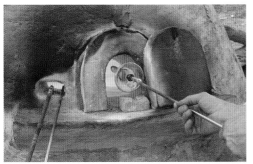

A small amount of hot glass is gathered from the furnace on the end of a tubular blowing iron and is shaped by rolling it across a flat surface made of stone or metal. The gather is inflated and the bubble is shaped. The partly-made vessel, or paraison, is continually returned to the furnace for reheating, enabling it to be inflated, shaped and decorated using wooden and metal tools.

When the main part of the vessel has been completed, a pontil iron – a solid metal rod – is attached to the base of the vessel using a small gather of glass. The vessel is detached from the blowing iron by cracking the glass, usually at the neck. This is done by creating a weak point in the glass – perhaps using a small drop of water – and tapping the blowing iron. Work can now continue on the vessel, forming the rim, and attaching handles and other decoration.

Once removed from the pontil iron, there is a small circular mark or scar on the base. This can indicate the original shape of the vessel, even when only a fragment of base remains. A vessel that has been pontilled is more likely to have had a fire-polished rim, rounded or folded, rather than a cracked-off and cold-finished rim.

1) The hot glass being shaped

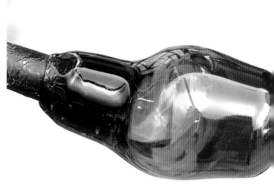

2) The first inflation to make the paraison

3) The paraison is extended

4)   and inflated to the required shape

5) Body decoration is trailed on at this stage . . .

6) . . . and the base is fashioned

7) Attached to the pontil, the rim is shaped . . .

8) . . . and handles can be added

HOW WAS GLASS USED IN ROMAN LONDON?

An urn used to hold the cremated remains of a Roman Londoner

Many types of glass vessels have been found in London. These show us that glass was used for a whole variety of purposes, such as at table for the serving of food, for drinking, and in kitchens and larders for storing and preparing liquids – wine, oil and water – and all sorts of foodstuffs. Bottles were even used as containers for liquids and other foodstuffs being transported over considerable distances, from one province to another. Small flasks and jars were used to hold ointments, medicaments and oil for the bath.

At the time of the conquest of Britain in the mid 1st century AD the finest tablewares and cups were made from brightly coloured glass and would have been made in distant places such as Italy. Later in the century vessels made in a clear, almost colourless glass became fashionable, sometimes with elaborately cut decoration to catch the light. These too were made in other parts of the Empire, and such vessels would have been costly and valuable items. At the same time, however, more utilitarian, everyday vessels were made from glass which appears in various shades of blue-green (depending upon the impurities in the raw mix), which is the natural colour of Roman glass. All these everyday items were of course made in other materials as well, such as pottery, wood, bronze or even precious metals, but although relatively expensive and breakable, glass had great advantages in that it was easily cleaned, it did not smell and did not taint the flavour or perfume of its contents. Glass was also used for windows, to make tesserae for the most elaborate floor and wall mosaics, for stirring rods, used with cosmetics and unguents, and for gaming counters, beads, pendants and hairpins.

A small oil flask for use in a bathhouse; a leather or metal handle would have been attached to the looped handles

Fragments of stirring rods, also a product of the London glass houses; these would have been used for mixing drinks and cosmetics

But glass could easily be broken and, when this happened, the broken fragments (cullet) could be recycled in a local glass workshop. It is interesting to consider that most of the complete glass vessels known throughout the Roman world, including Roman London, have been found in burials, where they were placed intact, containing food, drink or perfumes for the deceased. Broken glass may have had some monetary value to some people, but not so much that it would encourage them to desecrate cemeteries.

A clear glass beaker, now slightly discoloured, from the eastern cemetery of London

Gaming counters in opaque white and very dark, almost black, glass

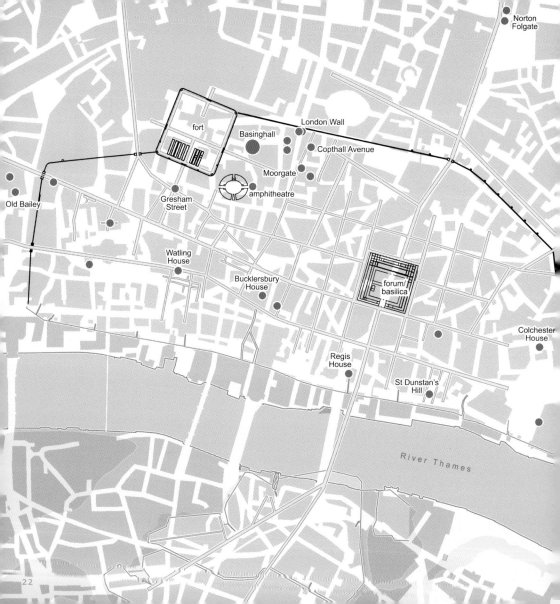

Norton Folgate

London Wall

fort

Basinghall

Copthall Avenue

Moorgate

Gresham Street

amphitheatre

Old Bailey

Watling House

Bucklersbury House

forum/ basilica

Colchester House

Regis House

St Dunstan's Hill

River Thames

HOW MANY OTHER SITES IN ROMAN LONDON HAVE EVIDENCE OF GLASS WORKING?

The glass-working zones of Roman London, showing the Roman road system (in yellow) and city wall, over the modern street plan; the concentration of red dots marks the upper Walbrook Valley with the Basinghall site on the its west side, north of the amphitheatre

Including Basinghall Street, there are now 21 glass-working sites known in Roman London. These are clustered in eight geographically and chronologically distinct areas. Not all of them were found recently – some discoveries were made as long ago as the 17th century, several were made in the 19th and early 20th centuries. It is only with the more recent opportunities for excavation in advance of development, and with improved techniques for both excavation and analysis, that we are able to take full advantage of the evidence. This is why the Basinghall Street site is so important.

The earliest evidence for glass working comes from the west of the city at Gresham Street, well outside the main focus of the contemporary settlement, where there is evidence for the manufacture of local pre-Roman style beads using recycled Roman glass, in the middle of the 1st century, before AD 70.

At a similar date, between AD 60 and 70, there is evidence for the first glass-blower in Roman London, indeed the first recorded glass-blower in Britain, working on the waterfront, on the site of Regis House. This is the only excavation to produce evidence for the actual position of the furnace, but the remains were so severely damaged by later occupation that little information was retrievable. The associated waste suggests that drinking vessels, small glass bottles and twisted stirring rods were produced. Located on the waterfront, in a warehouse, it is tempting to suggest that this glass-blower had travelled to Britain with his family and skills from abroad. Indeed, he was probably the first travelling glass worker to arrive in the country.

Two sites in the middle Walbrook area, Watling House and Bucklersbury House, excavated under extremely difficult circumstances in the 1950s, provided evidence of glass-working waste and cullet dating to the late 1st century. In the early 2nd century, c AD 120, a workshop, or series of at least eight small furnaces, was in operation to the west in the Old Bailey area, north of Ludgate Hill, perhaps remaining in use until the end of the century. The site was only partially excavated, again under extreme rescue conditions, and as the glass waste was identified only at the post-excavation stage, it was not possible to investigate the furnaces in any detail. There

Two beads, in a local non-Roman style, found among glass-bead-making debris at Gresham Street

are tantalising antiquarian records, by John Conyers, in 1677, of furnaces and possibly crucibles in the same area, near the Fleet ditch.

There is probable evidence of bead manufacture in the Newgate Street area in the early 2nd century AD, but the most important area for glass working at this date was the upper Walbrook valley, where there are no less than nine known sites, among which is Basinghall Street. This marshy area, crossed by many small streams, had been used as an industrial quarter on the edge of the as yet unwalled city from the late 1st

Two views of a fragment
of a glass-working furnace
found at Northgate House

century AD and was served by roads coming from the residential zones to the south. Modern redevelopment has afforded the opportunity for some extensive archaeological investigations and, although the number of sites on which glass-working waste was found may appear small, the volume is, in some cases, startling.

Some of the observations and records of finds in the upper Walbrook valley were made a long time ago. A note by William Newton, made in the late 19th century, records fragments of a 'glass-blower's floor' close to London Wall, and during the early 1980s small quantities of working waste and fragments of furnace were discovered on two London Wall sites and also at Copthall Avenue. Larger amounts were found widely spread over the site at Moorgate/Coleman Street with no obvious concentrations, but the first substantial evidence came from another Moorgate excavation close by. This site produced many fragments of objects and structures related to the glass-working

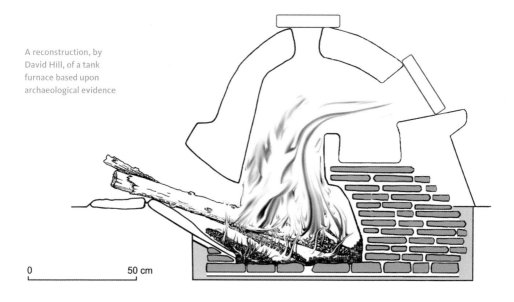

A reconstruction, by David Hill, of a tank furnace based upon archaeological evidence

0   50 cm

industry. In particular, they included some large glass-covered fragments of brick and fired clay, which have been identified as the suspended brick base of a tank furnace and part of the vertical clay wall of a furnace. At Northgate House, Moorgate, further along the modern street to the south, glass waste, furnace fragments and a quantity of vessel fragments were discovered in pits very close to a number of pottery kilns. This material from these two Moorgate sites is very similar and probably comes from a common source.

The glass-working waste from Guildhall Yard, when it was first discovered in 1992, was the most impressive collection ever found in London – or indeed anywhere in western Europe. A shallow pool or pond, which had formed following the collapse of a drain outside the eastern entrance of the amphitheatre, had been backfilled with rubbish, including huge quantities of broken vessel, window glass and glass-working debris, intended for recycling. This cullet weighed about 50kg, estimated at over 100,000 individual fragments, and it is thought to have been collected and dumped during the time of the Emperor Hadrian, c AD 120–40.

A comparison between the Guildhall material and the glass from Basinghall Street shows that the waste fragments are very similar, with a large collection of glass waste from the ends of glass-blowing irons (moils), threads and droplets formed during the vessel making processes, and other fire-distorted vessels and fragments. There is also a wide range of vessel glass among the Guildhall cullet dump, with a greater proportion of bottle and window glass than that found at Basinghall Street. One important question remains unanswered for both the Guildhall and Basinghall Street sites. Just why was this valuable commodity, the recyclable glass, discarded?

After the 2nd century the glass-working industry seems to have moved away from the upper Walbrook valley and dumps of glass-working debris of late 2nd- or 3rd-century date were found in the south-east corner of the city during excavations at the Tower of London in 1955. The few furnace fragments found there suggest a technology similar to that used in the upper Walbrook valley, although the wide variety of moils might suggest a more extensive repertoire of vessels, and the quality of the pot or tank

metal is superior to that found elsewhere. Two other sites in this south-eastern area produced small quantities of waste – St Dunstan's Hill, investigated in 1967, and Colchester House, Cooper's Row.

The latest evidence for glass working, a dump dating to the 3rd or possibly the 4th century, comes from two sites excavated in the 1980s to the north of the city, in the Norton Folgate area.

The outstanding collection from Basinghall Street must, therefore, be placed within this overall picture of the Roman glass industry in London, which is gradually emerging – from its beginnings in the earliest days of the settlement to activity in the 3rd or 4th century. Its height appears to have been in the 2nd century, in the upper Walbrook area where the Basinghall Street site is located, and certainly this was a period when there was a great demand for glass vessels, both as everyday household items and as containers for redistribution and storage.

One important observation is clear – namely that at all times glass workshops were, sensibly, sited on the marginal areas of the town. In such locations, they lay beyond the main area of development and, as the city grew, it is only logical to suppose that the glass workers, and indeed other craftsmen, moved their workshops to peripheral areas as the city expanded. But one more question needs to be posed – were there always glass-blowers in London or, having fulfilled specific local contracts, were they travelling craftsmen who then moved on to other towns, returning at some later date to London to continue their work? If so this may explain why there is no long-established glass workers' district in Roman London.

Trays of glass fragments from the cullet dump found in the area east of the Roman amphitheatre being washed by one of the authors on site

WHAT EXACTLY WAS FOUND AT 35 BASINGHALL STREET?

The site at 35 Basinghall Street was excavated by MOLA between 2002 and 2006 in advance of redevelopment. It is situated on the western edge of the upper Walbrook valley, with the Roman (or, as it is commonly known, Cripplegate) fort further to the west, and the amphitheatre to the south-west. It lies on the fringes of a marginal area, away from the main focus of residential settlement, where there was little activity before the beginning of the 2nd century AD. Before the start of the excavation at Basinghall, the upper Walbrook valley was known to be an area of industrial activity with evidence for a major pottery workshop on the eastern side of modern Moorgate. There was also evidence for leather working and, most significantly, a 2nd-century glass furnace on the edges of a canalised Walbrook tributary, suggesting that this part of town was occupied by small workshops which made use of undeveloped land, with its plentiful supply of water. Following the discovery of the large dump of cullet outside the eastern entrance of the amphitheatre at nearby Guildhall Yard, it was always hoped that more evidence for glass working would be found at Basinghall Street.

London around AD 120, just when the glass workers became established in the Upper Walbrook area; the Basinghall site is marked

The reality far exceeded expectations. There was only a little evidence for buildings, which seem to have been barns or sheds, perhaps for the storage of materials associated with nearby industrial or horticultural activity. Most of the site was covered in pits, used for quarrying of brickearth and, subsequently, for the disposal of domestic and industrial rubbish. In the south-east corner some of the pits contained over 70kg of glass production waste – in excess of 10,000 fragments. Unique among London assemblages, the waste found at Basinghall Street comes from all stages of the glass-working process. By studying this waste in considerable detail we hope to answer questions about the original sources of the raw materials and how the glass was prepared, the techniques used to produce glass vessels, what types of vessel were being made, the scale of the operation, its duration and its date. This will involve, among many other things, categorising and weighing the entire assemblage, even the individual vessel fragments. Some questions can only be answered by chemical analysis of selected fragments and batches of glass. Although there was no evidence for any associated structure or furnace, the material seems to be the debris from a failed tank of glass, perhaps rubbish thrown out when a workshop was abandoned.

Domestic debris, ceramic pots and bones, thrown away into a ditch alongside the glass workers' workshop

RIGHT One of the authors working on the Basinghall material; the many thousands of fragments had to be sorted by hand into their different categories of colour and waste type before being more closely examined

WHAT DID THEY USE TO MAKE THE VESSELS AT THE BASINGHALL WORKSHOP?

Chunks of raw glass from the furnace

At Basinghall the material from which the vessels were blown can be grouped into two main categories, large lumps of glass and cullet. Some of the large fragments are chunks of clean blue-green glass similar to those found on some Continental sites and it is just possible that these were originally imported as larger blocks or ingots – a question that may be resolved only by chemical analysis. Some fragments are extremely small and it is possible that they have been crushed before being put into a crucible or tank for remelting. The other fragments appear to be tank metal from the furnace, two fragments weighing over 6kg each. It was normal for the glass or tank metal that accumulated during the lifetime of a furnace to be broken up for recycling when the tank was dismantled, and its presence in such large quantities here suggests the cessation of the industry on this particular site.

The larger fragments are dark green in colour, but there is some variation and they contain distinctive white spheres, which formed as the glass cooled slowly. Most of the fragments of tank metal are much smaller, but there exists a single mass of glass, found in a separate pit, that is half a metre across and weighs about 30kg. This appears to have flowed from a tank furnace, perhaps over a period of time, as several distinct 'horizons' within the mass of glass are visible; the piece also shows the crystallisation caused by slow cooling.

Other large blocks of crystallised glass show details of the inside shape of the furnace

A large block of tank metal that has crystallised, being excavated

A fragment of window glass still with mortar, used to secure it in place, still attached to it

Nearly 4kg of cullet, consisting of broken glass vessels, was also recovered from a single pit, and substantial quantities came from other contexts. Most is naturally coloured blue-green glass largely from thin-walled vessels, but there are significant amounts of colourless glass and some fragments in dark blue, amber and yellow-brown. There are also many body fragments of thicker bottles and window glass fragments, a natural choice for cullet as bottles and windows contain a large volume of glass. Several pieces of window glass were clearly reused, either mortared or grozed (trimmed) to fit a window. This shows that some window glass had been collected as cullet and not made in the workshop.

In addition to these bottle and window glass fragments, at least 400 individual vessels can be identified by form. These are chiefly tablewares, such as bowls and jugs, or containers, a variety of jars and phials, with relatively few drinking vessels. Forty beakers and cups that can be recognised include some good quality vessels in colourless glass. The general character of the group, with very few fragments of 1st-century forms, suggests that it dates from well into the 2nd century AD.

Also found were some lumps that comprised partially melted layers of window glass, which are now fused together. This is perfect evidence for the preparation of cullet on this site.

A mass of fused window glass fragments ready for recycling

WHAT IS THE EVIDENCE FOR BLOWING GLASS VESSELS AT BASINGHALL STREET?

The glass assemblage contained large amounts of production waste. This was found with the vessel cullet and was also intended for recycling. The most significant of these is the moil, the small cylinder of glass left on the blowing iron after the vessel has been detached. Most of the glass working sites known from London have produced small numbers of moils, typically fewer than ten, but at Basinghall Street over 1500 complete or near complete examples have been identified individually, with a further 4.5kg consisting of over 6000 moil fragments. Most are in naturally-coloured blue-green or green glass, but there is a small though significant quantity of colourless, amber and dark blue examples – each complete moil represents a single vessel in these colours. Moils are, therefore, diagnostic evidence of the manufacture of glass vessels and suggest that, although we have no evidence for the structure of the furnace itself, the workshop was nearby.

A newly blown vessel in Mark Taylor's workshop, still attached to the blowing iron

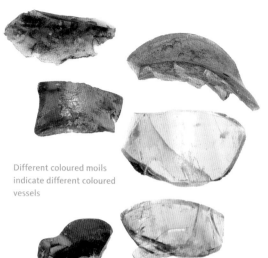

Different coloured moils indicate different coloured vessels

Some of the moils show crizzle spots, crazing of the glass where it has come into contact with a drop of cold water that had been dropped onto the hot glass to help crack the vessel from the blowing iron. This creates both the distinctive crizzle spot on one side of the cylinder of the moil and also a slight step in the profile of the moil on its opposite side, a feature which can be seen on many of the examples. At the other end of the moil, where the glass was wrapped around the iron, there is a characteristic ridge, which makes it possible to identify moils from extremely small fragments.

Many thousands of moils, each representing a single vessel, have been found in the workshops of the upper Walbrook valley

A colourless moil showing a crizzle spot

Several fragments are entirely crazed, suggesting that, after the vessel was removed, the end of the blowing iron was plunged into cold water to remove the moil.

The moils vary greatly in size; some are very long, others extremely short. Both the length of the moil and the degree of overlap around the blowing iron suggest that the glass-blowers were using different, perhaps individual, techniques and we may, by detailed examination of each fragment, be able to identify batches of vessels, or perhaps the idiosyncrasies of individual craftsmen.

Using a wooden stick, a drop of water is placed on the hot glass creating a crizzled spot – a weak point that will break the vessel from the blowing iron

Most of the moils are cylindrical, produced in the manufacture of narrow-necked vessel forms, such as phials, or jugs, and open vessels with folded rims, but a number of lid moils in colourless glass were also found. As their name suggests, these are lid-shaped and come from vessels with wider mouths and cracked-off rims, such as cups and beakers. The lid moil was removed from the vessel when cold.

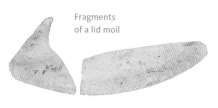

Fragments of a lid moil

Short and long moils from the Basinghall site

A mould-blown vessel made by Mark Taylor and David Hill, still with its lid moil attached (right), and a vessel with it removed (below)

RIGHT Large solid impurities in the glass can be pulled out of the glass before blowing

Fashioning a base

Applying a trail around a neck

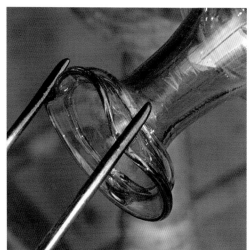

Forming a spout

Adding a handle

On at least 50 fragments, typically small flattened roundels of glass with pincer or pinch marks, distinctive tool marks have been recognised. Many are attached to threads and trails of glass, and experimental work suggests that some were the piece of glass discarded after handles had been attached to the body of vessels, such as jugs or bottles; they were dropped onto the workshop floor or put into a collection bucket for remelting with the other cullet. Some discarded fragments of similar shape contain stones, small specks of clay or other impurities, and seem to have been produced when the these particles were hooked out from the gather – a form of quality control.

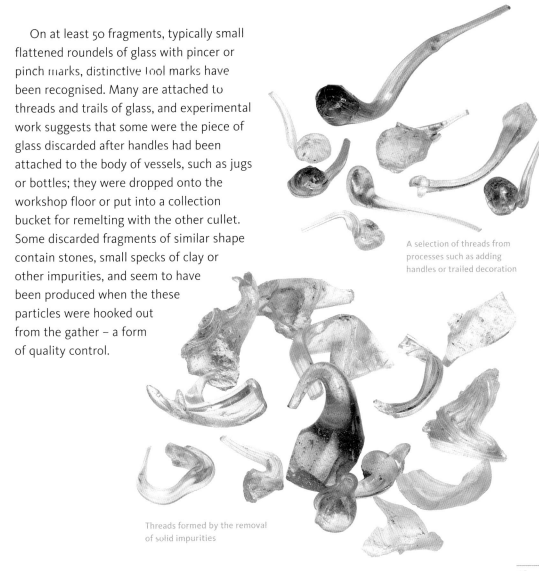

A selection of threads from processes such as adding handles or trailed decoration

Threads formed by the removal of solid impurities

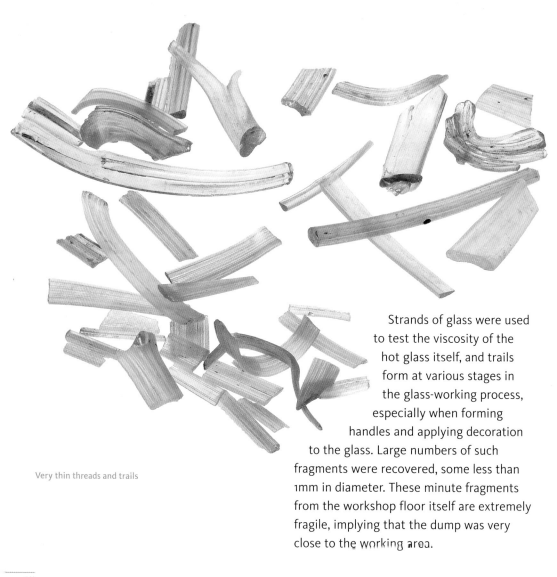

Very thin threads and trails

Strands of glass were used to test the viscosity of the hot glass itself, and trails form at various stages in the glass-working process, especially when forming handles and applying decoration to the glass. Large numbers of such fragments were recovered, some less than 1mm in diameter. These minute fragments from the workshop floor itself are extremely fragile, implying that the dump was very close to the working area.

What is the molten waste?

A large quantity of misshapen molten waste was found. Much of this was formed in the furnace itself, raked out with the hot ash from the firing, and was probably swept up from the workshop floor. Depending upon its condition, such material may have been collected for recycling, but some pieces are so 'dirty' that they are obviously genuine waste. Some of this formed large dribbles and runnels.

A bucket of wasters and cullet from a modern experimental workshop

Waste Roman glass from Basinghall Street that has come into contact with the fire of the furnace itself

DO WE KNOW WHAT SHAPES OF VESSEL THEY WERE MAKING?

It is difficult to work out the forms of the vessels being made from the size and shapes of the moils alone. Their diameters are irrelevant as the rims are often worked after removal from the blowing iron – both narrow-necked and wide-mouthed vessels could be made from similarly sized moils. It is likely, however, that the longer, cylindrical moils come from the manufacture of vessels with narrow necks, such as jugs or flasks. The vast majority of the moils and wasters are in naturally-coloured blue-green glass, often of rather poor quality, and it is likely that the workshop produced a range of utilitarian household wares intended for the local market. The cullet contains vessels of other colours, such as blue and colourless fragments, but this waste could have originated from anywhere in London. However, of more significance among the cullet are coloured and colourless moils. This can only be production waste, suggesting that a wider range of better quality vessels was made at some stage in the life of this workshop or another nearby. The wider lid moils, all in colourless glass, may be from cups or beakers.

Some of the waste, as we have seen, is identical to that produced by experimental glass-blowers when attaching handles or applying decoration

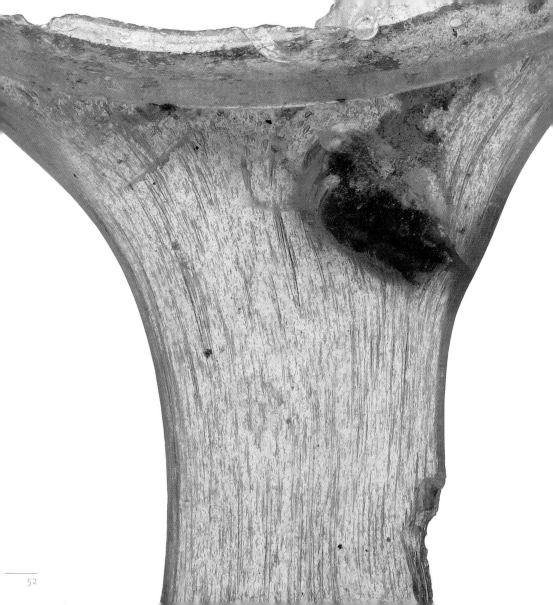

WASTERS?

It is probable that some of the fragments of cullet are wasters, typically misshapen vessels or mis-blown fragments which have been discarded for remelting. Many of these rejects are made of very bubbly glass. When cullet is melted for recycling and heated to a high temperature, the bubbles and other impurities which rose to the surface could be skimmed off, leaving a good quality clear glass for blowing. The presence of many tiny bubbles (seed) and black specks (batch) in the blown vessels suggests that the cullet was heated to a lower than ideal temperature. This by itself is useful evidence to show that the Basinghall glass workers may not have been able to construct the most efficient of furnaces.

Detail of a waster from Basinghall, showing poor quality glass

AND WHAT WAS THE SCALE OF PRODUCTION?

Put simply, every individual moil that can be identified represents a single glass vessel. These moils and other dumped waste material are unlikely to have been moved far from the working area, so detailed examination of the moils, counting and measuring every single fragment, will give us some idea of the total number of vessels that were produced. We may never know how long it took to collect all the cullet, but an examination of how the layers in which the cullet was found accumulated – whether over a short or long period of time – will assist us here. We are severely hampered by the lack of furnace evidence – one all-important measurement we are lacking is the volume of glass contained within the furnace – but comparisons with recent experimental work will give us an indication of the daily output of a furnace. In addition, the detailed study of the different techniques represented on the moils just might suggest how many workmen were employed. One important fact, however, is clear – this glass workshop was not a small-scale manufacturing site, but was responsible for the production of a considerable quantity of glass for use in London and, perhaps, beyond.

A short moil still attached to the blowing iron from a modern workshop

AND WHEN?

It is a reasonable assumption that the cullet we have found was collected over a relatively short period of time, perhaps over just a couple of years, and close examination of the vessels within it should give some indication of the date. The vessels are mostly in blue-green glass – bowls and jugs for use at table, with some storage jars and phials – but there are also some good quality colourless drinking vessels which came into vogue in the later 1st and early 2nd century AD. There are very few fragments of ribbed (pillar-moulded) bowls, heavy cast and sagged vessels which were extremely common in the 1st century AD. Being made of thick glass, these bowls were highly suitable for recycling and appear in quantity among the Guildhall yard cullet dump. The absence of these vessels suggests that the cullet dates from well into the 2nd century AD, when the ribbed bowls, made by more laborious non-blown techniques, were no longer fashionable.

A 1st-century AD ribbed bowl; these vessels were in use into the first years of the 2nd century but their absence from the Basinghall site shows that they had long gone out of fashion before the workshop was started

WHO WERE THE GLASS WORKERS?

Sadly, the individual glass workers in Roman London, their names, where they came from and what status they had in the town, remain a mystery. Indeed, there is very little evidence anywhere else in the Roman world, although occasionally names are recorded on (mould-blown) glass vessels and on tombstones. We can make some suggestions about the status of the London glass workers. The fact that glass-working sites, as at Basinghall Street, are on the margins of the town, or in areas which were not yet developed, is perhaps logical, as glass working was a potentially dangerous operation, with the ever present possibility of fire. It was just the sort of operation which would fit well into an industrial area of pottery kilns and smelly industries such as leather tanning. There is no need to reconstruct a large building for the site of the furnaces because, as today, workshops would have been quite small and contained. But these artisans, gathered together on the fringes of the town, might also have found themselves on the margins of society. There is little doubt that they were competent craftsmen, capable of creating well-appreciated products, but to what extent

were they integrated into the social fabric of the town? It is possible, in fact it is quite likely, that artisans such as glass workers were peripatetic – moving from one town to another in pursuit of custom. This might explain why the evidence for glass working in Roman London moves from one part of the town to another as time progresses – because as each successive group of glass workers arrived in the town, they would set up their workshop in a different area.

A wooden stick being used by Mark Taylor to fashion the handle of this replica Roman vessel

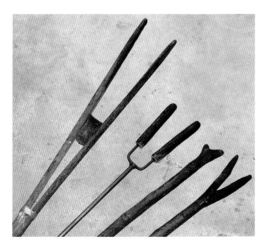

The glass workers of Basinghall Street, therefore, might have travelled some distance – perhaps even from another province – before setting up in the upper Walbrook valley. We do not, yet, know for how long their workshop lasted   although it is likely to have been for only a few years, rather than decades. Having spent a period of time in London, making glass vessels for the citizens of the town, they might then have moved on to a new town – somewhere nearby or even back across the channel. And behind them they left the last traces of the last few days of their craftsmanship – broken glass vessels and waste from their production which they never managed to use – which then became scattered across the site for the MOLA archaeologists to discover 1800 years later.

Wooden tools are common in glass workshops, but they do not survive for us to find

WHERE NEXT?

The main phase of recording and analysis of the glass-working waste from Basinghall Street is only just beginning and we are still finding new evidence as we examine the fragments in exhaustive detail. At present we can only pose questions. Some will remain unanswered but, with every new discovery, we are afforded tantalising glimpses into the little-known workings of an important industry and its craftsmen.

Experimental work has taught us a great deal about how vessels were made and what processes the different types of waste originally came from, but there are still many unanswered questions

FURTHER READING

J Bayley and J Shepherd, 1985 The glass-working waste, in G Parnell, The Roman and medieval defences and later development of the Inmost Ward, Tower of London: excavations 1955–77, *Transactions London Middlesex Archaeological Society* 36, 72–3

W Gudenrath, 1991 Techniques of glassmaking and decoration, in H Tait, *5000 years of glass,* 213–41, London

J Keily and J D Shepherd, 2005 The glass, in F Seeley and J Drummond-Murray, *Roman pottery production in the Walbrook valley: excavations at 20–28 Moorgate, City of London, 1998–2000,* MoLAS Monograph Series 25, 178–86, London

J Keily and J D Shepherd, 2005 Glass working in the upper Walbrook valley, in F Seeley and J Drummond-Murray, *Roman pottery production in the Walbrook valley: excavations at 20–28 Moorgate, City of London, 1998–2000,* MoLAS Monograph Series 25, 147–55, London

J Price, 2005 Glass-working and glassworkers in cities and towns, in A MacMahon and J Price, *Roman working lives and urban living,* 167–90, Oxford

J Price and S Cottam, 1998 *Romano-British glass vessels: a handbook,* Practical handbooks in archaeology 14, York

M Perez-Sala and J Shepherd, 2008 The glass cullet assemblage, in N Bateman, C Cowan and R Wroe-Brown, *London's Roman amphitheatre,* MoLAS Monograph Series 35, 142–6 and 202–08, London

M Taylor and D Hill, 2008 Experiments in the reconstruction of Roman wood-fired glassworking furnaces, *Journal Glass Studies 50,* 249–70

PLACES TO VISIT REAL AND VIRTUAL

Real

Museum of London Roman gallery
British Museum Roman galleries

Virtual

http://www.museumoflondon.org.uk/ceramics/
http://www.museumoflondonarchaeology.org.uk/English/ArchiveResearch/ArchiveOnline/
http://www.romanglassmakers.co.uk/